HOW TO WRITE AN AWESOME NOVEL

RICK WOOD

RICK WOOD PUBLISHING

Cover design by James at GoOnWrite.

Published by Rick Wood Publishing.

With thanks to my Advance Reader Team.

INTRODUCTION

A few years ago, a reader emailed me and asked:

I've attached five hundred words I've written. Can you read it and tell me if I have what it takes to be a writer?

I looked at this email for quite a while, shifting between despair and disbelief.

Firstly – who the hell am I to tell someone whether they can or can't be a writer?

No one has such a right. Not Ernest Hemingway or Charles Dickens or Stephen King themselves have any right to cast factual assertions over your work. Opinions, yes, but not a conclusion based on five hundred words whether you have what it takes to be a writer.

My reply said as such, and I also questioned... are these five hundred words a first draft?

She asked me what I meant.

I said, have you rewritten it, or just typed it out and expected instant perfection.

As it turned out, it was a first draft.

I said, in that case, you should not be showing me. First drafts are for your eyes only. Should you rewrite something and want advice on how to improve it, I would be happy to give you my opinion. But I would not be providing conclusions on first drafts, and I certainly would not be deeming whether another person can accomplish what I have, or something even greater.

At the time I was seeing success after success, and I suppose one could have forgiven me a bit of arrogance – a trait that is often debated as to its merits or disadvantages.

To explain, I want to take you back to February 2018. I was working as a teacher, and I hated it. Every morning I dreaded getting out of bed. I used to love the job but had grown to despise it.

This was also the month I handed in my notice. I would give up teaching that summer.

Why?

I was going full-time as an author. I would achieve my lifelong dream. I was giddy, a giddiness that saw me through to the end of July when I taught my last lesson and dismissed my final class.

In that time I also had my first bestseller. *The Sensitives* achieved the number one spot in *Ghost Thrillers* on Amazon in the US. It also achieved a bestseller spot in the UK, though I forget the category.

Everything was perfect. My books were growing my fanbase. Any stigma about being an independent author would be easily countered by the quantity of people who buy my books.

I remain, to this day, a full-time author. As I write this, in March 2020, I have had five books reach bestseller spots. I have published under two pseudonyms. I have passed my master's degree in Creative Writing with merit and have begun my PhD in Literary and Critical Studies, funded by loans and the revenue of my books.

This book is not about my successes, however, and at this point I will stop referring to them.

This book is about you.

Whether you are struggling to get that book done... Whether you have an idea but don't know where to start... Whether you've written a book or two but don't know how to make them better or where to go next...

Never fear.

This book can act as your guide.

It will be your tutor, but not your instructor. It is advice, as all creative teachings are.

Take nothing as a solid rule, even though I may state them that way.

Never see a mistake – instead, see an opportunity for learning.

And, most importantly, and most significantly – never, ever, ever let anyone tell you whether you have what it takes to be a writer.

You will know that yourself once you finish your book.

As often, finishing your book is all it takes.

PART 1

THE IDEA

CHAPTER 1

DEVELOPING YOUR IDEA

AH, THE IDEA.

Seems like a good place to start.

Often writers are bursting with dozens of ideas. Often writers struggle to come up with any. And, most of the time, we probably fit somewhere in between.

I will not tell you how to come up with a million-dollar idea. Honestly, there is no such thing.

As I will emphasise to you many, many times in this book, an idea is worth very little compared to that idea's execution.

What I want to help you with, however, is *blank page syndrome.*

You want to start writing, but where on earth do you start?

Sometimes our ideas need a nudge. Those 'eureka' moments you get when you are trying to sleep or sitting on the toilet – they only happen because you have spent time developing your ideas.

If you think of your ideas as the running of a car – your car only runs because you spent time maintaining it and putting in petrol. Your mind only works in the background if you have already fuelled it.

Your Approach to Ideas

As you develop your ideas, there are a few ground rules I would like you to follow:

1/ Do not omit ideas.

2/ Do not censor ideas.

3/ Do not force coherence to your ideas.

A bad idea may well be a bad idea. Or you may just see it that way. Or that bad idea may lead to a good idea. Either way, learn to be okay with everything not having to be perfect.

The belief that an idea is only worthy if it is amazing is counterproductive. It stops writers with fatal consequences. An openness to imperfection is crucial to creativity:

It is okay for everything not to be okay.

Do not expect perfection, as you will not achieve it. Instead, accept that your ideas and your work will be in a constant state of development.

So, if you need help to develop an idea you already have, or coming up with an idea, here are some exercises you can use.

What If?

We can condense every story into a *what if* question.

Some examples:

What if a neglected boy found out he was a wizard?

What if a girl fell for both a vampire and a werewolf?

What if two people fell in love just before the Titanic sank?

Hopefully, you will have guessed that I am referring to *Harry Potter*, *Twilight* and *Titanic*.

So, now you have a go. Get your notepad and write as many *what ifs* as you can.

If you have a story idea in mind, then come up with *what ifs* to develop that idea, such as: What if this character did *this*? What if this character went *to this place*? What if he fell in love with *her*? And so forth.

If you have no story idea, come up with *what ifs* about anything.

What if you grew a third boob? What if your house shrank to the size of a cup? What if your intestines could talk?

However stupid the idea, write it down.

Remember the rules – no omitting or censoring your ideas. And do this without stopping, with a target in mind – for example, try to write thirty ideas without your pen ceasing to move.

Once you have finished, have a look at what you have come up with and ponder on each *what if*, exploring where you could go with the idea.

Stream of Consciousness

This is where you write, often with a prompt, and continue

writing until your time is up. For example, put a timer on your phone for two minutes, then do not remove your pen from the page until those two minutes are up, no matter how incoherent and ludicrous the output is. You do not need punctuation; you just need to put all the thoughts in your head on paper.

To come up with new story ideas, you could use a generic sentence starter, such as *If I ruled the world...*

If you want more ideas about where to go with your story, come up with a relevant sentence starter. For example, if you were coming up with ideas for *Alice in Wonderland,* you may start with *If Alice went down the rabbit hole then...*

For Star Wars, it may be *If Luke Skywalker found out he's Darth Vader's son then...*

If you are writing a haunted house book, you could try *If a family lived with a ghost then...*

Once you have finished, look at what you've come up with. Explore it. Consider where each idea could go.

It may be a good idea for you to have a bit of a break until you return to what you've written. This will help you read your ideas without prejudice.

And / So What

Write a statement at the top of your page summing up what your story is about.

Then answer the questions *and* and *so what* again and again, until you have reached a set number of sentences or reached a time limit.

This will not only help you come up with ideas but will help you get to the crux of your story.

For example:

Luke Skywalker wants to go to the Death Star.

And?

And rescue Princess Leia.

So what?

Because it is important to him.

And?

And if he doesn't, he won't discover what he is capable of.

And there it is – the crux of the story. Luke Skywalker discovering what he is capable of.

What next?

Have a go at a few of these exercises. Try them out in

different ways. Be open to new ideas and never believe an idea to be a bad one.

Write lists. Create mind-maps. Do whatever you need to do to reach down inside of you, grab those ideas, and pull them out.

CHAPTER 2

GENRE

It is a common misconception to new and aspiring writers that the industry is crying out for something startlingly original to create huge ripples across the world of writing.

It is the unexpected truth, however, that both readers and publishers are after something familiar.

Of course, there have been books that have proven to be the exception. Books like *Harry Potter* that appeared unique inspired a whole generation of new readers. It is the case, however, that you are unlikely to write the next *Harry Potter*.

I do not say this to destroy your dreams and ambitions. Hey, maybe you will write the next big book! I say this to share the knowledge I have gained in how to sell books.

Publishers do not want you to send them something hugely original. They want you to send them something they can sell. And if you send them something unidentifiable to any book already out there, they will not know who to market it to. Similarly, if you publish independently, you will not know which audience to aim your book at.

Readers, too, crave the familiar. A reader will pick up a

crime book, not because they want to read something different to every other crime book out there, but because they are after a certain set of characters, certain story elements and a certain mood and tone.

Yes, we have big names who have published huge books unlike anything out there – but they are extremely rare. Most of us writers making a living do so through genre fiction. We produce books that follow the same tropes as the others in the genre.

Readers want to know what they are getting when they buy your book.

Similarly, I am often put off books that claim to have 'a twist you won't see coming,' and this is a good example of when some authors don't quite get it.

To those authors who put such a claim in their book's marketing and metadata, you are missing the point.

A reader does not want an impossible twist that completely stumps them. They want a twist that, when it happens, prompts them to say "ah, now that makes sense!" Regardless of whether they gain satisfaction from guessing the twist, they want the happiness of recognising how it all fits together.

This is not to say, however, that you can't use the tropes of a certain genre in an original way. Many books have done so, and I will share some examples shortly.

Before we do so, we need to ensure that we have agreed on a definition of genre. I will go with the definition as outlined in Cambridge Dictionary:

> *A style, especially in the arts, that involves a particular set of characteristics.*

To be more specific with the jargon we are using, I will refer to those characteristics as tropes. Here is the Cambridge Dictionary definition for tropes:

> *Something such as an idea, phrase or image that is often used in a particular artist's work, in a particular type of art, etc.*

Each genre has specific tropes. These are the elements required to fit that genre's conventions.

The originality of a book often comes out of the way you approach the tropes.

Saying this, I don't want to get too caught up with the concept of great, original ideas. People place way too much emphasis on the idea behind a story, often neglecting to understand that it is the execution of that idea that is far more important. It is, however, worth exploring what some tropes are and how existing authors have approached them with their own unique spin.

I will use the thriller genre and the horror genre to give some examples of genres and tropes, as this is what my experience of writing is in. This concept will still apply to the genre you write, and if you are unsure of the tropes of a particular genre, a bit of googling or asking the writer community should provide some answers – or, even better than this, you yourself using your analytical mind to note down the tropes you can identify will allow you to explore the genre with a far deeper understanding.

The Thriller Genre

General tropes of the thriller genre:

- Edge of your seat.
- Hurtling toward a climax.
- Villain-driven – an antagonist often provides the obstacles for the protagonist.
- Relies on suspense.
- Protagonist is often in dangerous situations where they are tested.

Subgenre: Espionage

Tropes:

- Uses an intelligence agency that is taken from real life, or based on real life, such as MI5 or the FBI.
- Has a 'big brother is watching' mentality.
- Involves agents on a mission.
- May have a deadly love interest.
- There is a time limit.

Subgenre: Crime / Noir

Tropes:

- Normally about a detective / police officer, or about gangsters.
- The protagonist is often an antihero.
- The law is normally a hinderance.
- Police procedures are expected to be realistic.

Subgenre: Political

Tropes:

- Set against a political power struggle.
- Uses issues of a specific time period, for example, the cold war or 9/11.
- Features corruption.
- Involves national and/or international scenarios.
- May often involve conspiracies.

Subgenre: Legal

Tropes:

- Driven by action in and out of a courtroom.
- Usually about criminal lawyers.

- The antagonist is normally corrupt.

Subgenre: Murder Mystery

Tropes:

- Is about finding a killer.
- There will be a set of clues.
- Everyone is a suspect.
- All the events make sense in the final big reveal.

Subgenre: Supernatural

Tropes:

- Set in the real world (if we set it in a constructed world, that would be fantasy).
- Often based around ordinary people who become aware of the supernatural.
- Involves people or creatures with powers of some kind.

Subgenre: Psychological

Tropes:

- Focuses on the characters rather than a large, intricate plot.
- It explores philosophical and ethical dilemmas.
- Can be seen as a 'light' version of horror.

The Horror Genre

General tropes:

- Involves shocks.
- Has evil, twisted characters, as well as vulnerable characters.
- Has disturbing scenes.
- The antagonist often represents something sinister about ourselves or the world.

Subgenre: Haunted House

- Involves a house that's old, with a lot of history – the house is often a character in itself.
- People move into this house, often a family, and experience things happening in a slow buildup.
- Research into the history of the house shows what kind of entity may be in it.

Subgenre: Vampire

Tropes:

- Usually fits into one of the following categories: vampire dystopia (such as *The Passage*), vampires as animals (such as *I Am Legend*), or vampires as immortals (such as *Interview With a Vampire*).
- Vampires drink blood and have fangs.
- Dependent upon category, the vampires either appear feral or identical to humans, and either live in secret or inhabit a new society.
- There's often someone who hunts the vampires.
- Whatever interpretation of vampires the book uses, it remains consistent.

Subgenre: Zombie

Tropes:

- Set in the onset or the aftermath of the apocalypse.
- Zombies usually arise out of either an infection or via supernatural means.

Subgenre: Post-Apocalypse

Tropes:

- Apocalypse is usually because of human actions.
- Dystopian apocalypse usually has some form of

society still intact, whereas in post-apocalyptic all resemblance of society has fallen.

- Normally follows a character trying to protect something or get somewhere.
- The humans that the protagonist comes in contact with are usually the biggest threat.

Subgenre: Occult

Tropes:

- Involves actions such as demonic possession, satanic cults and evil spirits.
- The victim is normally vulnerable.
- There is an expectation that time will be spent growing a relationship with the characters before the true horror begins.

Subgenre: Splatterpunk

Tropes:

- Contains extreme, gory violence and upsetting scenes of horror.

Subgenre: Children's Horror

Tropes:

- Focusses on the bizarre rather than the horrific.
- Short chapters.
- Mentor appears to be creepy and dangerous.
- Child has to go against authority to discover the truth.

Bringing Your Own Originality to the Tropes

As I have mentioned, using the tropes of your genre is more likely to create a book you can sell, whether to a publisher or to your readers directly.

This is not prescriptive, of course. If you believe you have something completely original that someone will want to buy, go for it. I am merely nudging you toward writing a book I know carries a statistically greater chance of success – and usually the tropes of your subgenre will help sell your book.

As I have mentioned, this does not mean you can't use these tropes in a unique or original way. Many authors have created original stories doing this and have often created new tropes that other authors now follow.

Here are a few examples.

Carrie.

This is a paranormal horror book. As the tropes dictate, the protagonist is vulnerable, and the antagonist is deadly. The originality came through making the protagonist and the antagonist the same person.

The Da Vinci Code

A thriller where the protagonist has a fascinating area of expertise. Dan Brown uses the tropes, however the situation the character is in and the puzzles he has to solve are unique to other thrillers. It is the fascinating information provided in the puzzle that often hooks the reader.

Interview with a Vampire

Before this book, vampires did not take on the characteristics of people. You could not have a civilised conversation with one. Take *I Am Legend*, for example, which was published two decades earlier. Richard Matheson's vampires were evil, feral, animalistic creatures (at first anyway – don't want to give any spoilers away!)

Of course, many books have been written since where vampires are more humanlike, but that's because this book paved the way for them to do so.

The Hunger Games

A young adult dystopian novel.

Just like all dystopian novels, there is some element of

society still intact, but it is broken. The conflict of friends having to fight each other brought some originality to this trope.

In fact, you will find a lot of young adult dystopian books that have been successful since containing some imitation of *The Hunger Games*. Have a look at the book covers in this genre, for example – have you noticed how they all now follow the same format as the cover for *The Hunger Games*? This is completely intentional. Similarly to how genres use tropes, book covers also take on the characteristics of the most popular books in that subgenre.

What next?

Now it is your turn. Find your subgenre, learn the tropes, and decide – how can I use these tropes in an original way? How can I put my personal spin on them?

I would not get caught up too much on having to have a sense of originality in your idea. Remember – it is the execution of the idea that matters.

There are plenty of books and movies out there that had great ideas, but the stories stank.

It is up to you to craft brilliant characters, not spend ages coming up with an impossible idea you think no one has ever thought of before.

PART 2

PLANNING

CHAPTER 3

RESEARCHING YOUR NOVEL

There are two types of research you may do as you approach your novel:

1/ Factual.

2/ Inspirational.

Factual research is research you do for information. You carry it out to ensure that the details in your book are accurate. For example, on what date did a particular event occur? Where is a particular place located? If you are a crime author, it may be to find out how long a body takes to decompose in specific conditions, or to know the police procedure in your country for a particular incident.

With the internet a few clicks away, factual research is far easier than it used to be. You can google the answer or ask your question in the appropriate social media forum. There are also books that can answer specific questions – for example, I am aware of a book written by a police officer on information that crime writers need to know.

Inspirational research, however, is not based on facts. I truly believe that, for creativity to go out, creativity must first go in. Finding inspirational research helps to feed our creativity and generate ideas. Most importantly, I think it gets us in the correct mood and mindset for what we are writing.

For example, when I am writing a book about someone suffering from demonic possession, you can guarantee that every evening after I've spent the day writing I will watch a demonic possession movie. This helps me to maintain the right mood and mindset for me to be in when I write my novel.

Places you can go for such inspiration are Netflix, TV, the Blu-ray store. You can read books within your genre, and you can find articles online. If you are writing a psychological thriller about a stalker, then there are thousands upon thousands of articles online written from the perspectives of those who have been stalked, and psychologists describing typical stalker behaviour.

Some of the best inspiration research you can do is, in fact, natural research. Research that requires little action on your part. This involves, quite simply, listening.

If you're in the café, and a couple are arguing a few tables over, eavesdrop. Listen to what kinds of things they say, and how they say it. Listen to what they are arguing about and listen to the subtext. What do you think it is that they mean that they are not saying? Is one not feeling listened to?

Then, when you come to write that scene in your romance novel where the couple fight, you have some great research to help write that scene.

I remember once, during a summer's evening walking the dog, a friend observed that it was a strange time of the day, as everyone had their lights on but their curtains open.

I was writing a book told in first person by a serial killer – that line ended up opening a chapter!

You can experience your character's experience second hand. You can never truly replicate someone's experience, but you can create an experience that helps you write about it more authentically.

Do you have a blind character? Wear a blindfold for the afternoon.

Does your book take place in a school? Ask a friend who's a teacher if you can observe a few lessons. Witness the kinds of things students do and how they interact.

Is your character a martial artist? Go to a martial arts class!

Please, however, do not endanger yourself or others in doing this. If a character gets shot, you don't have to experience that!

In doing this, you will find your *show don't tell* improving – which is an important skill I will touch on in a later chapter.

You will pick up on things that will unknowingly find their way into your writing.

You will describe things in a specific way that sounds far better than the generic, imagined description otherwise conveyed.

What next?

Walk into a room. Write down ten things you observe. Then write another ten. And another ten.

You'll find the first few things end up quite general, for example, the sofa is grey. The television is on.

The more you force yourself to notice more and more things, the more you will find yourself observing the smaller details that help build up a scene.

For example: The curtains are drawn. There is mould on the base of the door. One person is avoiding looking at their partner. The carpet has indents where a seat used to be.

This will help you to stop writing generic sentences like *the room felt unwelcoming,* and start writing more specific sentences that convey this with more skill – *The room was bigger than the furniture allowed. The thermostat hung off the wall. No one lifted their gaze.*

CHAPTER 4

DEVELOPING YOUR CHARACTERS

I HAVE HEARD IT SAID THAT A READER MAY BUY YOUR book for the story, but they will read it for the characters.

I mostly agree – except that the reader will still buy the book for the characters. In a decent book description, we describe the story in the way it affects a character. That is what a reader invests in.

Without decent characters, your story is nothing. Your idea is worthless.

Your characters, if they are thought out and developed, will write your story for you.

If something perilous happens to your character and your reader is not invested in them, they will not care. If there is a big plot twist that affects a character, it won't matter.

This isn't just true with protagonists. Consider how many people loved to see the Joker in *The Dark Knight*. In fact, consider how much any Batman film is based around the villains – it often tells their backstory more than Batman's.

Remember, *invested* is not always the same as *caring* or *liking*. I often see customer reviews where someone says, "I didn't like the character." What they mean is they were not *invested* in the character. Your character does not have to be likable.

In fact, a lot of the best characters aren't.

Character Exercises

Exercise 1: What do they want?

Your protagonist, as well as your antagonist, will always have:

1/ Something they want.

2/ A reason they want it.

3/ An obstacle, or obstacles, standing in the way of getting it.

Your story is about your character trying to overcome their obstacle, or obstacles, to achieve their goal.

An example:

1/ Want: Spiderman wants to defeat Green Goblin.

2/ Reason: The Green Goblin has threatened his family and his city.

3/ Obstacle: The Green Goblin is his friend's father.

All stories are based around conflict. If there is no conflict your character must face, then there is no story.

This includes both outer conflicts and inner conflicts. You may think a reader wants to see a perfect character get destroyed then pick themselves up again. In fact, your reader will engage far more with a conflicted character. A character with faults that they must overcome.

For example:

1/ Want: Bill wants to become a better father.

2/ Reason: He wants to stop his son from feeling ashamed of him.

3/ Obstacle: He has a severe alcohol addiction.

If Bill is a great father, then there is no conflict.

It is important that you know what it is your character wants and what their conflict is.

Exercise 2: Role on the Wall

Draw the outline of a gingerbread man.

Now, on the outside, write all the character's external characteristics. By this, I mean the things that people can tell by looking at them.

On the inside, write all the character's internal characteristics. Things people can't see by looking at them.

You may end up with something like this:

SEB

Smooth

Cheeky

Cares little for anyone but himself (Critically)

Good-looking

Loves women

Quick-witted

Doesn't like changing his lifestyle

Always looking to flirt

Wants to be good at everything

Easy going

Happy

Would rather not try than try & fail

Takes everything in his stride

Always thinking something

Knows how good-looking he is

Thinks [illegible] & [illegible]

Player

Arrogant

Cocksure

Wants to have fun

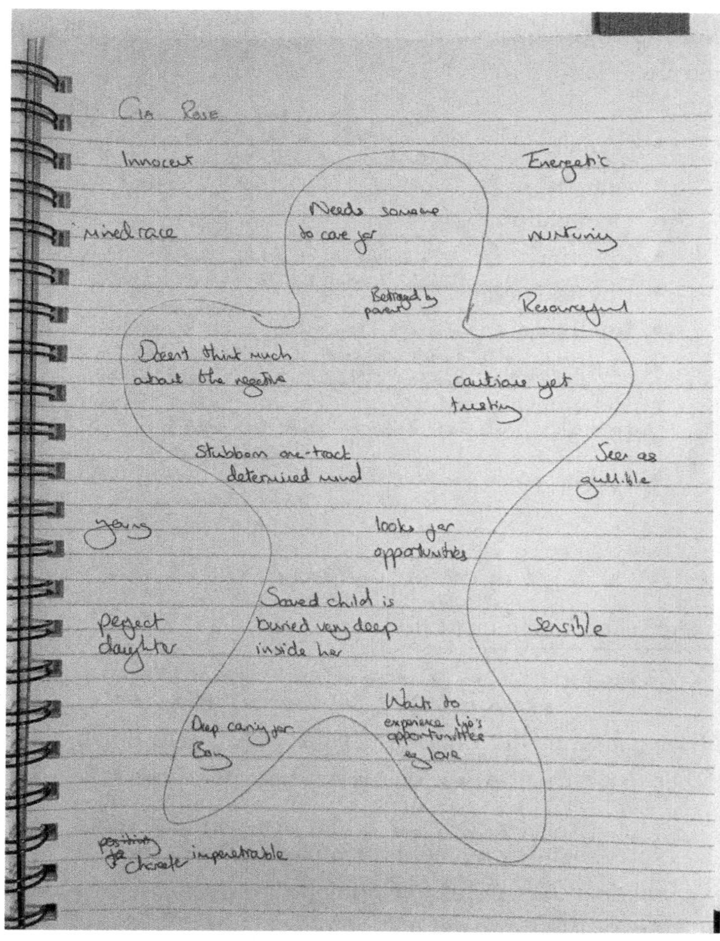

This gives you a far better understanding of who you character really is, and the face they present to the world.

Exercise 3: Key Information

Note down the key information about your character. This may include:

- Name.
- Age.
- Occupation.
- Location.
- Physical details.
- Intelligence.
- Outlook on world.
- Relationship history.
- Family.
- Habits.

Exercise 4: Timeline of Life

Draw a line in the middle of your page. Note down ages, either to death, or to the age your character reaches in your story.

Note down key moments of your character's life.

This may be useful for moments you can use in a non-linear narrative (something I'll discuss in more detail in a later chapter), but it can also give you a better understanding of why your character is how they are. A person's childhood shapes so much of who they are as an adult, and you will gain far greater sympathy and empathy for knowing this.

General Advice for Creating Characters Readers Want to Invest In

Saving the Cat

There are a few ways to help convey your character to the audience I have learnt through practice and further reading that I would like to share with you here.

The first one being the *save the cat* moment. This is a moment where your character does a good deed, such as saving a cat from a tree, hence the name. This moment is particularly important for an antihero, or a generally unlikable protagonist.

I would encourage you to make this moment organic, rather than forced. For example, do not have your character set out to rescue the proverbial cat from the proverbial tree – instead, make them have to stop what they are doing against their better judgement to save the proverbial cat.

For example, your disgruntled police officer could be on the way to get some whiskey. He is an alcoholic and hates the world and is desperate for that next drink. Whilst doing it, he notices a child begging in the street. He grumbles about it. When he is in the liquor store, he sees he has only a few quid, and the bread is there in front of him; so he gets the bread instead. He throws it at the kid, swears under his breath and moves on without the whiskey he so desires.

If the character set out to get the bread for the kid, that would be nowhere as effective as if he had to give up his task, and his drink, to help them. He still objects to doing it, even as he's doing it, but that doesn't matter, as his actions have spoken far louder than his words.

Motivation

. . .

You must force your protagonist into their predicament as the only one who can solve the problem – and in doing so, there must be some personal motivation. They must be invested in what they are doing, otherwise why would they bother?

If the detective is solving the crime because it's her job, where's the stakes? If, however, the detective is solving the crime because the girl who's missing is secretly the daughter she gave up at birth and she feels guilty for doing so – well, that is a far more compelling premise. That protagonist could not leave the situation simply by handing in her notice.

Similarly, if you are in a horror movie, and a lack of mobile phone signal or being locked doors is the only reason your character can't escape the haunted house or the killer, then there is not enough tying them to the conflict. It needs to get personal. Raise the stakes.

What if they can't allow themselves to go because they believe the killer might be their brother, and they just have to know the truth?

This is not to say that you should force motivation. If your character has too much, or indeed too little motivation, this can be damaging.

If the character is effectively motivated enough to chase the killer because the killer has their wife, you need not add halfway that the killer is also his lover, then add after another fifty pages that the killer also killed his family, then add after another fifty pages that the killer also used to be his brother but had a sex change.

An extreme example, but you can see what I'm saying – it's too much.

I dislike how, in the original Tim Burton *Batman* film, they revealed Jack Nicholson's Joker killed Bruce Wayne's parents. It isn't just that it's incorrect based upon the comic books (I'm a huge superhero geek), it just wasn't needed. Batman had his motivation; they didn't need to add this.

The motivation must be something that compels the character so the reader knows they have no choice, and that they cannot leave the situation. Nothing more, nothing less.

I would also advise against changing your character's motivation during the story, unless it fits. It can be done, but only if it is organic. Not forced just because the story needs it to be so.

Identification

Your reader will always pick a character to identify with. This won't always be the character you intended.

In my novel, *When Liberty Dies,* my main character was a Muslim girl hunted by a group of murderous racists. However, her boyfriend, the timid and shy Eric, was the one most readers identified with. This was completely unintentional.

Are you more likely to identify with the brave, noble, Harry Potter or his friend, Ron Weasley, who's always getting in messes and walking in the shadow of Harry?

Would you identify with Luke Skywalker, or his roguish friend, Han Solo?

Relatable moments will help your readers to identify with your character. These are moments more subtle than the *save the cat* moments.

For example, your character is hurriedly making tea and burns their hand on the cooker, making them late for their night shift.

Your character gets up, yawns, and stubs their toe on the door.

These moments are smaller. People are far more likely to identify with them. Saving the world and grand noble gestures are nowhere near as important to a reader as these moments.

What next?

Take your central character and try out the four exercises.

Once finished, consider how much more you know about your character. Consider how you will use what you know to write this character.

You may even want to stick your role on the wall and key information around your desk (assuming that you write at a desk!)

CHAPTER 5

STRUCTURING YOUR NOVEL

When it comes to planning out your story, there are two types of authors – planners and pantsers.

Pantsers are called as such as they write 'from the seat of the pants.' They do not plan, they just put their hands on the keys and write.

Planners plot out their story beforehand.

I am not an advocate for either approach. In fact, I use both dependent upon the novel. If I have a story that just starts with a situation and I want to see where it goes, I will pants. If I have a story that has a lot happening, then I will plan.

Planning removes some stress in your first draft. The blank page is often daunting, but if you have a plan written down then you already know what you will write that day. Without it, you are sitting at a keyboard with nothing to get you started.

I would definitely encourage you, should this be one of your first few novels, to plan. It will remove a lot of stress.

By planning, however, I do not mean that you need to

write a ten-page synopsis. It can be a page of notes, or you could use an excel spreadsheet. I have a noticeboard on my wall I plan my stories on. I use a memo pad for each chapter – meaning I can move, add or take away chapters as I go along.

Pantsing is also a lot easier when you instinctively have the typical story structure in your mind.

By this, I mean the three-act structure that 99.999% of stories adhere to. It is very rare you will find a film without this structure, although books are often more liberated from it.

I would encourage you to select which parts of this structure to use. My suggestion is that you learn the rules before you break them – know this structure, so you can use it should you get lost. Earlier on in your career, it might help to use this structure as a template then, as you progress, use it as a guide.

There are lots more parts to the typical three-act structure than I will give you here. My belief is that you need to know the main components, not every little detail, to avoid your story getting prescriptive.

The Three Act Structure

Act One is the beginning, which lasts a quarter of your story.

Act Two is the story world, which lasts half of your story.

Act Three is the resolution, which lasts a quarter of your story.

So, for example, if you had a 100-page story, it would be roughly something like this:

Act One – 25 pages.

Act Two – 50 pages.
Act Three – 25 pages.
Now let's look at how each act breaks down.

Act One: The Beginning

Hook

Sometimes the story will start with a hook, but not always. This is a scene that sets the tone and grips the audience. An example is *Harry Potter and the Philosopher's Stone*. The opening scene shows Dumbledore, Professor McGonagall and Hagrid delivering Baby Harry to the Dursley's, talking mysteriously about an event that has just occurred.

Similarly, every *James Bond* movie opens with a scene designed the hook the audience.

Ordinary World

Here, we see the protagonist in their everyday life. This is what their life is like before the story starts.

For example, Luke Skywalker buys some droids. Shaun from *Shaun of the Dead* gets up and yawns. Andy from *The 40-Year-Old Virgin* wakes up with an erection. Harry Potter makes breakfast for the Dursley's.

. . .

Call to Adventure

Something happens that breaks the protagonist out of Ordinary World and pushes them into the story.

Luke Skywalker sees Princess Leia's message on R2D2, or Harry Potter talks to a snake in the zoo.

This is followed by *Refusal,* where the protagonist tries to resist the call to adventure but is forced to by an *Inciting Incident.*

The First Trigger

An incident that completely removes the protagonist from their previous life, normally with a change of location or a drastic event. They could still potentially return to Ordinary World, but it would be tough for them to do so.

Luke Skywalker finds out that his aunt and uncle have been killed. Harry Potter receives his letter from Hogwarts.

Act Two: The Story World

Watering Hole

The protagonist goes somewhere to gain information that will help them on their quest.

Luke Skywalker and Ben Kenobi go to Mos Eisley to

meet Han Solo. Harry Potter goes to Diagon Alley to find out about Voldemort and the wizarding culture.

First Twist

There is a twist in the story. Perhaps the protagonist faces the antagonist for the first time and loses, learning just what they are up against.

Mid-Point

This is one of the most important parts of the story. This is when two things occur, usually with one event:

1/ Everything is revealed. For example, we see the villain in *Sleepy Hollow* for the first time. Luke Skywalker sees the Death Star for the first time.

2/ It is the point of no return. No matter what happens, they cannot return to Ordinary World any longer. In *Revenge of the Sith,* Anakin Skywalker turns to the dark side and there is no going back. In *The Hunger Games,* Katniss enters the arena.

With Call to Adventure, they were a little removed from Ordinary World. With the First Trigger, they were even further removed. Now they are completely removed and have no way of returning.

At the previous two points they could have returned, though it would have been tough – now they cannot return even if they want to.

. . .

Second Twist

A further twist in the story.

The protagonist will go through change. They will discover things about themselves and seek what they need to face their challenges and to overcome their obstacles. Use this twist to show the character growth.

The Big Slump

This is right at the end of Act Two, and it is rare you will find a story without this.

This is where everything is at its worse. The protagonist is as far from what they are after as they could be, and it looks like they have absolutely no hope.

In a romantic comedy, the love interest may have boarded a plane to another country. The protagonist has no way of knowing where they are and has let them go.

In a detective thriller, there are no clues, the killer has escaped, and the detective has no chance of capturing them.

Act Three: The Resolution

Divine Intervention

Something happens that breaks the protagonist out of the big slump.

The protagonist suddenly realises how they feel about the love interest and decides that they will race to the airport to stop the love interest leaving.

The detective suddenly realises what a clue meant from earlier and knows how to catch the killer.

A mentor teaches the protagonist something they knew all along.

The Final Fight

The big fight at the end. This could be a fight between the good guy and the bad guy, or it could be the race to the airport to find the love interest.

This normally concludes with the *Resolution*.

Return to Ordinary World

We see how the protagonist is now.

The story is over, and we discover their new world.

In *Harry Potter*, Harry boards the train back home.

In *Shaun of the Dead*, he goes into the shed and plays video games with his zombie friend.

My Process

I will share how I plan out a story, and it may be a way you wish to try.

I write every event I wish to happen in the story on sheets from a memo pad. I keep writing and writing until I have all the events in my story in front of me.

I will then arrange each sheet into the order I wish for those events to occur.

I will look at the story in front of me and add any more events that I need to fill in any information, gaps, or needed characterisation.

Finally, I pin all the sheets on my noticeboard, and it will look something like this:

What's next?

Take your ideas and note down the story events you would like to happen.

Can you arrange these ideas in a way that follows the structure?

What might you need to add? If you find you are missing a first trigger, for example, add a story event that fulfils it. Continue doing this until you have a plan in front of you.

PART 3

THE WRITING PROCESS

CHAPTER 6

YOUR FIRST DRAFT

So many writers fail to write a magnificent story as they do not understand the fundamental concept being the process of creating it.

So many times, I hear the same complaint – "I write something, then I read it back, and it's just awful." Or, "Everything I write is rubbish," or, "I keep deleting it and going over it."

Is this you? If so, you are failing the realise the important, unequivocal, unobtrusive truth:

All first drafts are awful.

I will repeat this, so I can batter it into your head as much as I can:

All first drafts are awful.

Stop reading it back and judging yourself on it. Stop deleting it and stop going on about how terrible it is.

Remember, once again:

All first drafts are awful.

Your first draft is the hardest part of writing. It is the only part of the process where you are looking at a blank page, expected to vomit words upon it. If you expect all those words to be perfect at this stage, then you are missing the point.

Your first draft should be written for yourself, and should be written without editing.

The first draft is about getting it done. That is all. Set yourself a word count – mine is 3,000-5,000 words a day, but when I first started, it was 500-1,000 words. Make it realistic. And stick to it.

You are just creating something that you can later craft into a decent novel; not something that will be readable first time.

Never, ever show anyone your first draft.

Shannon Hale put it best when she said that your first draft is you pouring sand into a sandbox so you can later build sand castles.

You can't create those sandcastles without a big lump of sand first.

If you wish to change something as you go along, don't. Keep momentum. Instead, keep a notepad by the side of your computer (or whatever you use to write on.) If you have an idea, note it down and return to it in your second draft.

This will often happen when you realise you needed to add a bit of information earlier on to make what you are writing make sense. Note it down and return to it after.

More than anything, the first draft requires discipline.

If you don't do it, you won't be a writer.

No one will buy a book you didn't write.

No one will make you do it but yourself.

Don't expect to always feel creative. Don't expect to write perfection.

Just force yourself to sit down and do it. If you write 1,000 words every day, then you will find yourself with a 60,000-word first draft in two months.

Not bad, eh?

Embrace the awfulness. Accept the atrocity. Come to terms with the dire product you will create.

Just write it.

Now.

Go!

What next?

Set yourself a routine. Be disciplined. And write the worst first draft you possibly can.

CHAPTER 7

THE PROCESS OF REDRAFTING

I THINK A LOT OF ASPIRING WRITERS GET CAUGHT UP ON the quality of their first draft because they aren't actually sure how to go about the redrafting process.

It is your job, once your first draft is done, to craft it into something readable.

Again, don't expect to finish this on the second draft, or even the third or fourth. It is a process.

Once I have used the second draft to make any changes I noted down for myself in the first, this is the cycle I then use:

- Start big and zoom in.
- Get feedback.
- Start big and zoom in.
- Send to copy editor.
- Publish.

By 'start big and zoom in' I mean that, at first, you look at your novel as a whole, then get a bit closer on each draft.

So, for example, you may use draft 3 to look at the structure of your novel. You may use the next draft to look at the structure of each chapter. You may then use the next draft to look at the prose.

Then you get feedback – as, by this time, you will have gone over your work so much you will have no idea what is and isn't working anymore. This can be a developmental editor, or a trusted friend, or someone in the creative writing community.

Once you have feedback, use that feedback to go through this process once again. I independently publish, so I would then pay a copy editor or proof-reader to check my work for mistakes once this whole process is complete.

So your process may well look like this:

Draft 2 – put notes into action.

Draft 3 – look at the structure of the novel.

Draft 4 – look at the structure of the chapters.

Draft 5 – look at the quality of your prose.

(Get feedback.)

Draft 6 – structure of the novel.

Draft 7 – structure of the chapters.

Draft 8 – prose.

(Copy editor)

Draft 9 – final changes.

How to Redraft Your Structure

Get a notepad, preferably A4. Write the chapter number, then a short sentence describing what happens on one line. Miss a line, then carry on with the next chapter, until you have your novel outline in its current state in front of you.

This may seem like an excessive amount of work, but it

won't take you that long. It will allow you to be able to look at your story as a whole.

Now, as you gaze upon your story, you can scrutinise it. Here are some questions you may want to ask yourself:

- Are there any chapters that aren't adding anything to character or plot and should be removed?
- Are there any chapters that should be added, whether to add information or develop a character further?
- Are there any chapters that would be better off at a different place of the story?
- Does anything strike you as needing to be fixed?
- Does the story keep its pace?
- Are there any inconsistencies, whether in character or in information?
- Do you have your Chekov's Gun moments? (I will explain this later.)

In different colours, annotate your outline with what you need to redraft.

Here is an example from one of my stories:

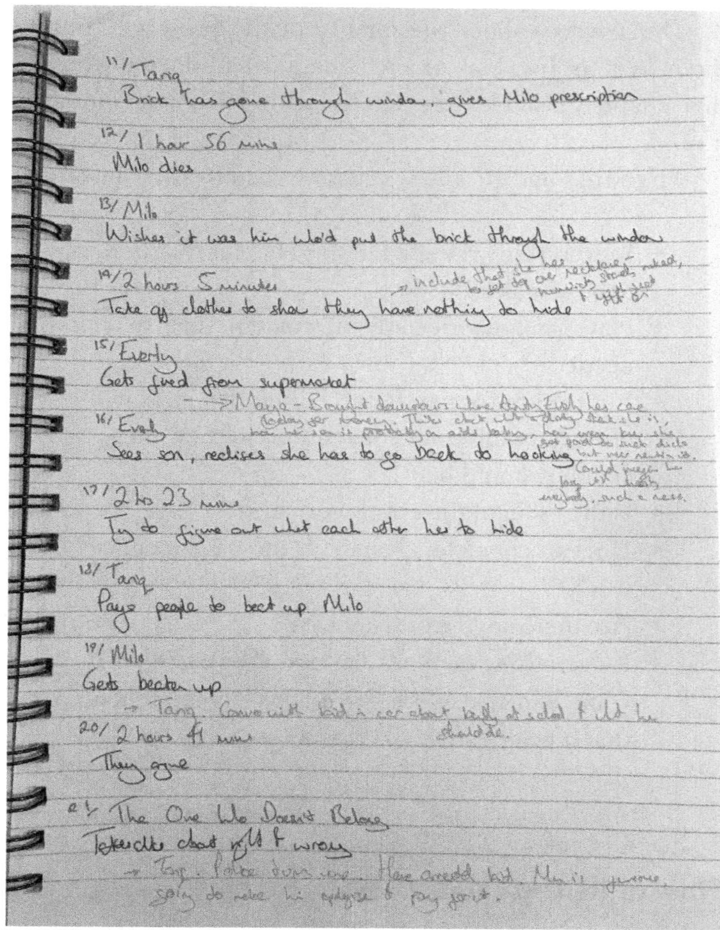

11/ Tariq
Brick has gone through window, gives Milo prescription
12/ 1 hour 56 mins
Milo dies
13/ Milo
Wishes it was him who'd put the brick through the window
14/ 2 hours 5 minutes
Take off clothes to show they have nothing to hide
15/ Everly
Gets fired from supermarket
16/ Everly
Sees son, realises she has to go back to hooking
17/ 2 hrs 23 mins
Try to figure out what each other has to hide
18/ Tariq
Pays people to beat up Milo
19/ Milo
Gets beaten up
20/ 2 hours 41 mins
They argue
21/ The One Who Doesn't Belong
[illegible] chat right & wrong

How to Redraft Your Individual Chapters

Now, take each chapter in turn and analyse the information in it.

Don't worry about the quality of the prose yet, that is the next step. Just look at each chapter and decide whether that chapter provides the reader with what you intended it to.

Here are some questions you may want to ask yourself:

- Is everything revealed in this chapter that needs to be revealed?
- Have you provided any information that isn't needed?
- Is it too long or too short? (Different genres will often have different conventions for how long a chapter should be.)
- Is the order of the events correct?
- Do your characters behave as those characters would?
- Are there any inconsistencies?
- Is everything factually correct? (For example, if your character uses a gun, have you researched that type of gun?)

How to Redraft Your Prose

By prose, I mean your effective use of language and the clarity of your writing, such as sentence structure, use of show don't tell, syntax, dialogue and so on.

You need to consider why you are using particular words, whether you convey the correct amount of tension, and what your language says about each character.

The next chapter will focus specifically on developing

such skills, but here are some questions you may want to ask yourself:

Are you using clichés?

Remove all phrases, clichés and idioms. It's cheap writing. There are always better ways to describe things. If you use a cliché, then you are basically telling your reader you are too lazy to think of your own way of conveying some information.

Clichés are often too generic. Consider other ways you can write that sentence that is more specific to your characters and your story.

For example, imagine reading the following sentence: *He and his sister were like chalk and cheese.*

It tells us nothing, really. Sure, it suggests the siblings don't get on, but it's told in the same way as any non-writer could tell it. You are better than that.

Why don't the brother and sister get on? What is it they fight about? How do they act?

Be more specific, for example: *He and his sister always wanted the same toy at the same time, no matter what toy it was. Honestly, it was the only time she ever saw him after a Barbie.*

You learn so much more about the characters, and it conveys it in a more satisfying way for the reader.

There is an exception, perhaps, when one acknowledges the cliché in the writing as being a cliché and twists it, perhaps in an ironic way. For example, instead of writing, *he was the thorn in his side*, you could use it, such as *he was the thorn in his side, if the thorn was a bloody dagger and his side was his throat.*

Consider, also, writing clichés. By this, I mean things used by writers so often that they have become a cliché.

The most common writing cliché is a character looking in a mirror. Often when a character has a period of reflection, the character will look at themselves in a mirror and describe what they see. Not that there's anything wrong with this, and I know I'm guilty of using it, but it is worth considering a way you could convey this information in a way it isn't so typically conveyed.

Do you use words other than *said*?

Contrary to what we're often taught in school, words other than *said* should be used sparingly.

Consider the following dialogue tags:

- He bellowed.
- He consoled.
- He cautioned.
- He rebuked.
- He soothed.
- He asserted.

All lovely words, but are over-description.

Take *he bellowed* for example. Why are we not already assuming that the character is bellowing? Why haven't you already conveyed this information to the audience?

Instead of adding fancy dialogue attribution, consider instead what you have written in the paragraph before the dialogue.

For example, instead of:

. . .

"This is ridiculous!" he bellowed.

Try:

He pounded his fist upon the table and kicked the falling plates at the helpless cat.

"This is ridiculous!" he said.

Do you repeat words excessively?

We all have words we overuse.

After you've written a few books, you'll know what yours are.

For example, my overused words are *that* and *eyes*.

I am always writing about people looking at other's eyes. Similarly, I seem to pollute all my writing with the word *that*.

So, in my redrafting, the sentence *he looked at the cat that sat there quietly* could be changed into *he looked at the cat sitting there quietly*. It gets rid of a commonly used word and sounds much better.

If you are using Microsoft Word, press CTRL+F and type in your most common word. Now go through each use of the word and consider if there is a better word you can use.

Alternatively, use software like *Pro Writing Aid* and it will tell you which words you are overusing.

. . .

Are all of your words used in the right context?

Are you using the correct word for the context of the sentence?

It's easy not to, and can be difficult to notice. This is something my copy editor often picks up on, and each time I wonder how I didn't see it when I redrafted my work.

To use an example from one of my redrafts, I wrote the sentence: *He'd neglected a coffee, opting for whiskey.*

My copy editor pointed out my incorrect use of the word *neglected.* And she was right. How did I not notice that? The word is being used incorrectly. Instead, I changed it to: *He'd rejected a coffee, opting for a whiskey.*

Do you overuse adverbs?

Many authors despise adverbs. Stephen King in particular speaks out against adverbs. He detests them.

Personally, I think a good adverb has its place. But they can be overused.

When looking at an adverb, consider: If you took that adverb away, would you lose anything? Or would it tidy up the sentence?

Often – in fact, most times – you can take away the adverb and not lose anything in doing so.

An example is the sentence: *He sighed hesitantly.*

If you removed the word *hesitantly,* would it take anything away? Are we not assuming if he sighs, he does it hesitantly? Is this not already conveyed in your description?

If you removed it, the sentence would be far tidier.

. . .

Do you need all those words?

We tend to explain things in more words than we need to, and this phase of redrafting is a good opportunity to reduce the amount of words you use.

The best way to tell if you are using an excessive amount of words is to read it aloud. Does it sound too waffly?

Sometimes we add words we don't need. For example: *I grabbed the door handle with my hand.*

Do we need to know I grabbed the door with my hand? Are we not assuming? I mean, what on earth would I otherwise be grabbing it with?

That sentence then becomes: *I grabbed the door handle.*

Another example: *The arms of the patient.*

Let's change that to: *The patient's arms.*

Is everything consistent?

This is something I've suggested you look out for at every phase of redrafting. Honestly, it is the first thing a reader will criticise.

Some of these are obvious. For example, is the colour of the teapot the same? Is it red in one chapter then blue in the other?

Consider the actions and dialogue of your characters. Are they consistent with that character?

. . .

Do you use Show Don't Tell?

Actions speak louder than words.

This is especially true with your characters.

Show Don't Tell means you are showing or conveying something to your reader, rather than telling them. It is integral to good description and good writing.

In fact, I would probably go as far to say it is one of the most important skills you learn.

Don't tell us a character is sad or angry. Show us this.

Here is an example of a poor sentence from the second book I ever published:

He looked at a photograph on the fireplace with an aura of happiness.

I mean, I think it's probably the worst sentence I have ever written. It is awful, and one of my customer reviews on Amazon pointed it out quite brutally.

What if I'd shown that the photo was happy instead?

It could have been:

He looked at a photograph of a family on the beach, arms around each other, smiling.

Readers dislike being spoon-fed. They like to figure things out for themselves, and they will appreciate a sentence like this that allows them to figure out the photograph is happy on their own.

So, instead of writing that your character is feeling a certain emotion, always consider how you can show us instead. How you can convey it with their actions, or even their demeanour.

Instead of telling us of a person's characteristics, show us.

Don't tell us they are snobbish: show us them acting snobbishly.

Don't tell us they are over-enthusiastic about everything: show us them acting over-enthusiastically.

Are you information dumping?

Information dumping is when you blurt out lots of information to your reader.

Avoid it.

Too much exposition creates clunky writing.

Convey information only if it is organic to the character's line of thought. Information needs to be given to the reader naturally, rather than listed to fill in the gaps.

For example, here is a paragraph that information dumps:

Shane stood next to Tony. Tony was a wizard of the highest order, and he decided who could become a wizard and who couldn't. He also had a lot of magical powers.

Now let's look at how we can convey this information in a more natural way:

Shane looked at Tony, wondering if he would ever reach the level of wizardry that Tony had, and whether Tony would allow him to do so. It would, after all, be Tony's decision whether Shane became a wizard. Oh, how much he envied Tony's powers.

. . .

I have conveyed the same information; I have just made it organic to Shane's thoughts. Therefore, I am not just throwing facts at my reader; I am conveying them from the character.

Can you describe this in a way it hasn't been described before?

How many times have you heard someone's story or process described as a *journey*?

How many times have you heard someone call a group of people going somewhere *pilgrims*?

How many times have you read about a *tree swaying peacefully in the breeze*?

Yes, it works. But it works with the hundreds of other novels that have used these descriptions too.

How can you rewrite that sentence with a sense of originality?

An example:

We left the house on a journey to find hope.

Vs:

We stumbled out the house, searching for hope like a discarded paper bag searching for absence on the wind.

. . .

Which of these two is more interesting? Which conveys the style of voyage better?

Are you being too specific, or not specific enough?

Are your descriptions leaving enough to the reader's imagination?

You want to provide specific detail that suggests characteristics to the reader, not specific detail that dictates what they should think.

You do this by being specific about things such as items and places, but be less specific about physical descriptions.

Take *Carrie* by Stephen King, for example. At no point are we told whether Carrie is blond or brunette, slim or overweight, or has blue or brown eyes. Yet, we have a clear picture in our mind of what she looks like. This is because King describes her as a social outcast. This allows us to form our own image based on what we identify as a social outcast.

The exception is if a physical characteristic is relevant. If your character has one leg that will become a point of contention later on, then it is important to let your audience know this.

Being specific about items and places, however, tells us a lot about a character.

For example, consider these two sentences:

He sipped on his Blenheim Lead Crystal Panel Square Spirit Decanter and relished the sting of the Dalmore 62 Single Highland Malt Scotch, before turning to his medium rare steak.

. . .

Vs:

He sipped on his McDonald's strawberry milkshake and turned back to his cold cheeseburger.

If you had just written *he ate food and sipped on a drink,* that would not tell us much about the character or the situation.

Being specific about the items the character is using has helped us to convey two very different experiences in two very different sentences.

Is your point of view correct?

If you are writing in first person, is everything told from that character's perspective?

If you are writing in biased third person, is the telling of the story biased toward the character who is experiencing it?

(More on point of view in the next chapter!)

What next?

Once you have finished your first draft, use the start big and zoom in method to redraft your work.

Remember, all I have said is advice, and not unbreakable rules. Adapt my suggestions to your own style.

CHAPTER 8
WRITING TECHNIQUES

In this chapter, I will share with you some beliefs and philosophies about writing. I will share ways to improve your writing and mindsets to approach.

As I have already said, these are not set rules. Anyone who tells you there is a set way you have to write something is wrong.

So, take the advice that works for you, discard advice that doesn't. These are all things that have worked for me in my writing career, and it may be different for you.

With that said, let's have a look at a few aspects of writing.

Creativity

Creativity rarely arrives when you want it.

In a perfect world, we would sit down to write and creativity would arrive. We would place our coffee down, open up Microsoft Word, and there it would be, waiting for us, and the words will just pour out.

Whilst those days can happen, it's rare.

And, if you want to get your book done, you can't afford to wait for it. If you go more than one or two days without writing your first draft, you may lose momentum.

If you wait to feel inspired, you will get nothing done.

It is all about mindset. Often you will have a block.

What do you do when you have a block?

Power through.

Help yourself to be creative. Remember, for creativity to go out, creativity must go in.

Writing a book set in Brazil? Stick pictures of Brazil all over the wall where you're writing. Writing a paranormal horror? Watch a paranormal horror every night.

Either way, just write.

Whatever you are feeling, write. Even if it's awful. (Refer back to my chapter on the first draft!)

It is my belief that striving for perfection is the enemy of creativity. To be creative, you must remove the concern of making a mistake.

Remember, you aren't making mistakes – you are *learning*.

My favourite quote ever is by the UFC fighter Conor McGregor:

"I never lose – either I win, or I learn."

And, in the spirit of this, I want to share with you a book I wrote:

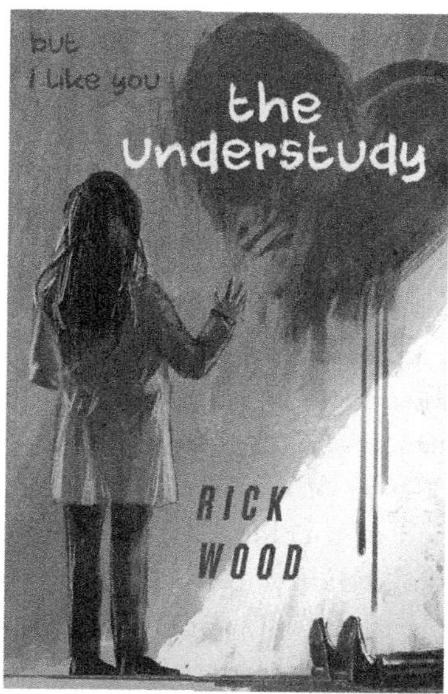

You won't find *The Understudy* anywhere.

Why? Because I unpublished it.

I think it was the fourth or fifth novel I published. And it was awful.

It had some fans who enjoyed it, but ultimately, it was terrible, and did not go down well.

But it was the most important book I have ever written.

From that book, I learnt far more about writing than my thirty or so other books.

It is okay not to be perfect.

And, remember, perfection is subjective anyway. Even the best books in the world get poor reviews.

Eight Rules to Follow or Not Follow

. . .

1/ Avoid contrived plot.

Readers will not forgive a flimsy plot.

If the protagonist needs to learn some new information, have them learn it during a bad experience.

Make sure the plot is always relevant to the character.

I rarely come across someone who doesn't feel cheapened by the ending of *War of the Worlds*. This is because, when the aliens all died of a cold, it was nothing to do with the protagonist. The plot didn't link to them in any way.

Compare this to the alien invasion movie *Signs*. In the end, an allergy to water defeated the alien attackers. The girl had left glasses of water out throughout the story that she refused to drink. The outcome was relevant to the character.

2/ Ensure you include The Big Slump

Out of all the structure points, this is crucial.

Your final battle will feel less satisfying without it.

You need to have the downs to have the ups.

3/ Motivation needs to be clear

Make your character's goal, motivation and obstacles clear early on.

Even if the reader isn't consciously aware that they are aware of them, they still need to be aware.

4/ Show Don't Tell

Don't tell the reader, show them.

He was angry.

Vs:

He barged a stranger off the bus, grumbling at the amount of space he was taking up.

5/ Be wary about swearing

Nothing wrong with it, but it can put readers off.

It's not so bad in television and film, as we hear it. Seeing it written is something else.

Use it, but sparingly.

6/ Challenge your characters

Your story is centred on conflict. Your protagonist will not entertain your reader if they have an easy ride.

Challenge your characters – both externally and internally.

Even if their beliefs and values are noble and/or integral to the plot, still don't let them go unchallenged. Don't be scared to make them confront the flaws in their point of view.

7/ Your characters must change

Readers love character growth.

The contestants who normally win reality television shows are the ones who have grown over the course of the series.

They must go through a change as a result of their experience, even if the core of the character remains the same.

8/ If you are stuck on plotting...

Come up with an ending and work toward it. It's far easier with a target.

Point of View

This is the perspective through which you tell your story. It is an important decision, as it will shape how the information is presented to the reader.

It is also tedious to go back and change after you've written a whole draft in one point of view.

Here are the different points of view you can go with.

First Person

The story is told through the character's perspective, from the point of view of "I."

Everything must be told through that character's eyes, even if you don't agree with it personally.

A great example of this is *My Sister Lives on the Mantelpiece*. It is told from a ten-year-old's point of view, and he doesn't understand what is happening – though we, as a reader, understand the reality of what he describes.

Similarly, *American Psycho* is told from the point of view of a deranged psychopath who murders people. We don't agree with his perspective (or at least I hope you don't), but the information is presented in a very different way than it would be should Patrick Bateman not be telling the story.

Multiple First Person

This is often told through different chapters from different character's perspectives. It can be interesting to see how these alternate points of view see the same events.

A great example is *Girl 4*, where we see events from both the serial killer's point of view, and the police officer hunting him.

. . .

Third Person Biased

The most common form of third person, told from the point of view of "he," "she," and, "they."

You don't go as deep into the character's mind as you would in first person. Still, each chapter is biased toward a specific character's perspective. It is not a good idea to go into one character's head then into another's in the same chapter. Instead, start a new chapter biased toward the next character's perspective.

Third Person Omniscient

This is where there is no bias toward any character, the story is just told.

I struggle to think of an example, and I don't recommend using it. Your reader will find it more satisfying if there is a bias toward a character.

Second Person

This is where the story is told through "you." It is rare to find, and many attempts to do this have failed.

The most successful attempt was through the *Choose Your Own Adventure* books where the reader is choosing what happens next.

The magnificent book *You* by Caroline Kepnes is a great example of a book that shifts between first and second, as the character telling the story addresses the reader as if we were the woman he's obsessing over.

Your decision

Often, your genre will have the expectation that you use a specific point of view. For example, young adult is usually written in first person.

The decision, however, is ultimately yours. It is up to you to decide which will tell your story best.

Style

Style is a difficult topic to teach, as it is so inherent in a person's writing.

Consider, for example, how everyone can speak... yet everyone's voice sounds different.

Most of us can write a letter... but no one's handwriting is ever the same.

Even though we are all writers... we have our own style.

It is difficult to imitate another author's style, just as it is difficult to consciously control our own. It is not something that is often deliberate.

When friends and family read my books, they always say they can hear me speaking in them, and that the words sound like they are coming from me. But, when I ask them how, they find it difficult to articulate.

However, figuring out the characteristics of your style is

still useful. Once you learn what your style is, you can develop it and enhance it.

Your style can end up being what makes you stand out from other writers.

Style may or may not be shown through your use of:

- Syntax
- Imagery
- Tone
- Tense
- Narrative style
- Point of view
- Language use

Your influences will affect your style. For example, Quentin Tarantino movies are usually a mash up of movies he loved. Part of what you read and watch will end up finding its way into your writing.

To identify your own style, you need to explore your instinct. What do you do with words and story? What common traits remain consistent throughout your writing?

To help with some examples, I have tried to identify aspects of my style, and have come up with:

- I often use a non-linear Then / Now narrative.
- When a character is breaking down, I use a stream of consciousness with little punctuation to convey this.
- I use researched mythology in my horror books.
- I often have single line paragraphs and short sentences.
- I use extended metaphors in single line paragraphs.

- I usually use deep third person biased.
- I often have flawed male characters and kickarse female characters.

The strange thing is that, looking at this list, I can see some things people hate about my writing. In my negative reviews, these are often referenced.

In contrast, however, these aspects of my writing are mentioned far more in my positive reviews. This is evidence that your style will not be for everyone – but will be for your tribe!

Let's look at my use of style in this paragraph:

He looked at her like she was a juicy lollipop.

A coveted sweet.

Sticky and appealing

She hated it and she loved it at the same time. It hurt. It hurt a lot. But damn, she hated to love it.

And when he began he began and he did not stop stop please wait what you are doing what are you–

God, she hated him.

Not a great paragraph, I will admit. But one that helps me demonstrate the elements of my style that I have identified.

When the character breaks down, I remove punctuation. I have single line paragraphs for emphasis. The first three lines are all the same extended metaphor. And it is deep in third person biased.

Chekhov's Gun

. . .

This is a theory that will get you out of many plot holes and dead ends. It is a perfect way to stop a moment feeling contrived.

It is the theory that if there is a gun on page five; it is because it will be fired on page ten.

You can replace the gun with whatever you need it to be. But planting that gun earlier on, or whatever item or information you need, means a character can use it later.

If a character suddenly pulls out an item that rescues them from a tricky situation, your reader will feel cheated. However, if you have shown the reader this item earlier on, then it feels satisfying.

Often, I will add an item that my character uses in my first draft, then make a note on my pad to go back and add it earlier on when I address my second draft.

Chekov Gun moments are particularly good for when the character is in The Big Slump and they need Divine Intervention.

Let's look at some examples.

Example A

Character A is in a fight with Character B and losing – you are not sure how Character A will get out of this fight.

The solution is to go back in the story and show a fight move that Character A was working on, but couldn't quite get right.

Now, when Character A tries that fight move and finds

that he is successful, the reader will be pleased to see this character's progress.

Example B

The love interest has left, and your protagonist is angry at them, but you need them to go from being angry with the love interest to missing the love interest. You aren't sure how to make this transition happen without it appearing contrived.

Earlier on in the story, add a pair of dorky glasses that the love interest was wearing. This became a big joke between them, and a moment where the protagonist felt like they were falling in love.

Now, when the character is angry and they come across those glasses, the anger can turn to sadness.

Example C

The detective has lost the killer with no idea how to find them, and you aren't sure how to get them out of that rut.

Plant a cigarette at one of the crime scenes earlier on that the detective acknowledges then dismisses.

As the detective bemoans his luck, have him notice someone else smoking. He abruptly remembers that cigarette. It is of the same brand as his friend – a brand that is only available in a certain part of the city. Boom, he knows where to look for the killer!

. . .

Linear Vs Non-Linear Narrative

A linear narrative is a story that is told in a chronological order.

A non-linear narrative is one that goes back and forth.

Having a flashback is different to a non-linear narrative. A single flashback to explain something often feels cheap. Can you think of a better way to convey the information?

A non-linear narrative, however, is one that goes back and forth throughout. Often, the Then chapters inform the Now chapters. You can have parallel plots running. You can use foreshadowing. It can also lead to a satisfying sense of irony.

Be wary, however, about going between past and present tense in your writing. This is a risky thing to do and often makes a reader feel unconsciously confused. Saying that, I did this once, and I quite liked the effect.

There is misconception that a non-linear narrative doesn't have a beginning, middle and end, or that it can't use the three-act structure. In fact, it is more important to have a sense of beginning, middle and end. Even though the narrative doesn't follow a straight narrative, it can still follow the same structure.

Most stories are told with a linear plot. It is still, as ever, up to you to decide on the best way to tell your story.

Dialogue

A lot of writers find this difficult. My belief is that, if you have developed your character sufficiently, their dialogue will usually come naturally.

We all have our own idiolect, and different groups have their own sociolect. If you know your character and their relationships, a lot of this will become instinctive.

It is still worth exploring how to write decent dialogue.

One of the most common questions is accents, and whether you should spell out words in an accent phonetically.

It's tempting, but it is really unpleasant to read. If I wrote a British northern accent as *"Are y' goin' dahn town?"* for the whole novel, this will get really tedious.

So how do you convey an accent?

Use dialect and idioms from that region. For example, someone who's Scottish may say, *"Would you like a wee drink?"*

This is far easier to read than spelling out all the sounds of the accent.

Similarly, people often say erm and er, but it isn't pleasant to read lots of verbal fillers. Using punctuation as beats is also a good idea, but not if overdone.

In terms of what is said in the dialogue, always consider the subtext. Humans never, ever, ever, ever say what they mean. If you have a character walk into a scene and say, *"I am angry that you slept with my brother,"* it would be wholly unrealistic. Instead, consider saying this in the subtext of their dialogue: *"Well, it sounds like you and my brother had a good time last night. What did you get up to?"*

We can use dialogue to break up continuous scenes of action – but do not use dialogue to fill silent gaps. Even in literature, silences can tell us a lot more about a character and a situation than filling it with dialogue can.

Allow your characters to have their own voice. Just don't fill it with excessive words, unless this is important to the character. Often, we can remove the first tag-on phrase of dialogue and lose nothing, for example:

"I think it would be easier to say no."

Vs:

"It would be easier to say no."

Setting

Before you describe the wind in the trees, or the torn wallpaper, or the way a random stranger walks, ask yourself: *is it relevant?*

Reasons it might be relevant are:

- The wind in the trees is pathetic fallacy, representing the windy nature of the scene.
- The torn wallpaper may reflect the shattered marriage that lives within the house.
- The way a random stranger walks may be important because the protagonist is scared, and everyone seems weird.

Reasons it may not be relevant are:

- The wind in the trees is weather that has no

impact on the character's actions and no reflection of their state of mind.
- The torn wallpaper is in a house of which the state has no relation to the scene.
- The random stranger has nothing to do with the protagonist.

If you are describing every detail of a room, ask yourself why. Over-description can be off-putting. We've all read books where we've skipped a paragraph, not interested in what it's saying.

Instead, give a sense of setting, then let the reader's imagination fill in all the gaps.

The right amount of specific details can tell us everything we need to know.

For example, what kind of person lives in this house:

The walls were beige, the rugs were a fluffy pink and a framed picture of a cat sat on the mantelpiece.

From this, we will know what the rest of this person's house will look like. We don't need any more. We already know spending an afternoon in this house and with its owner will probably be unbearable.

Consider again what kind of person lives in this house:

A bowl of Werther's Originals sat next to the pot-pourri. The curtains were sickly brown, and the television was so loud one had to shout to be heard.

Here, we can all picture a grandparent's house and fill in what the rest will look like with our imagination.

Theme

. . .

The theme, or themes, is the underlying idea or ideas of the story, and are usually implicit.

The theme will be a recurring subject or topic. It can be what the story is truly about, whether that be redemption, vengeance or blood. This is often unintentional at first and is something that you can emphasise as you redraft.

It is important to identify, as it gives your story a central focus, connecting the various elements. Without a theme, your story would be a bunch of events; the theme gives the reader something to connect these events.

Some often used themes are:

- Love
- Death
- Redemption
- War
- Good vs evil
- Growing up
- Violence
- Courage
- Prejudice

Some examples could be:

- *Carrie* – blood.
- *When Liberty Dies* – prejudice.
- *Kill Bill* – vengeance.
- *Da Vinci Code* – science vs religion.

When redrafting your novel, pick out a theme that has found its way in, and consider ways you can emphasise this in other parts of the book.

Some questions you may want to ask to help you identify your theme(s) are:

- What are your character's motivations?
- What is the story's conflict?
- What research have you done for your story?

Rhetoric

The rhetoric is language designed to have a particular effect on your reader.

Every word you use will have an impact, often unconscious. Make sure each word has its purpose.

Consider what is being implied beneath the surface, why you are using one word instead of another, and whether the words have the effect intended.

For example:

The rain came down like tears.

Vs:

The rain came down like bullets.

All I've done is change one word, but the impact of the sentence changes completely.

Similarly:

It was a fiery rage.

Vs:

It was a crippling rage.

Is the rage useful or not? If it's fiery, it could be. If it's crippling, then it's hindering her. The impact of the rage changes dependent upon the word used.

Series Writing

Why should you consider writing a series?

Thinking about it from a business approach, it makes sense. Your readers may well be invested in you as an author, but they would far more likely be invested in your series.

If you are planning on independently publishing, writing a series will be integral to your business model. I lose money advertising *The Sensitives*, but I make far more than my investment back through people who purchase the next seven books in the series.

People will often buy a Lee Child book because Lee Child wrote it – but I guarantee that, should you go back in time, people were originally more likely to buy his next book because it was a *Jack Reacher* book.

I thought it was worth mentioning a few mindsets you can adopt when you come to write a series, as it may well be what you end up doing.

A common series type you come across is a trilogy – three books following the story of a character, or characters. Sometimes a series with over three books will still be segmented into their individual trilogies, such as *Star Wars*.

This is a format they often follow:

Book One: Can often standalone. It is an introduction to the story world and the story conflict. It is a setup for the rest of the series, though usually ends in a way that can act as a conclusion or be continued. This is because publishers and film studios like to see how well the first does before commissioning two more.

Book Two: Is often darker. We raise the stakes. The acts are more destructive. The end usually has a hefty cliff-hanger, or a sense that the quest still has a way to go yet.

Book Three: Is the resolution. The final battle where the lessons are learned. The characters have a bigger skill set and, as a result, the battle is bigger.

You may well end up writing over three books in your series. For example, *Harry Potter* was written in seven. Many series don't have a foreseeable end and just keep going, such as *Jack Reacher*.

Here are some things you may wish to consider when approaching your series:

- Does your story develop in each book, or will each book be able to standalone?
- Will you tell each book from the same point of view? This is usually the case, though fellow paranormal author Shani Struthers has been very successful in telling each of her *Psychic*

Surveys books from a different character's point of view.

- Will you also release prequels and companion novels?
- If your story is continuous, do your characters grow in each book? Is the character growth consistent with that character?
- Are you ensuring that you don't just keep writing the same story?
- Do you keep the same genre and tropes throughout?
- Will you be able to keep your passion and interest in these characters and this story for a long period of time?

What next?

I have just dumped a lot of information on you – so don't sit there with a headache going over all the many skills you need to gain... these skills will develop with time and practice.

Have these ideas in the back of your head as you write your first draft, but do not fixate on them. Instead, use these as ways to improve your writing when you come to rewrite.

Perhaps, having read this chapter, it would be a good time to go through some of your written work and redraft it with these skills in mind.

And, remember – even though these may be phrased as instructions, they are suggestions. Anyone who tells you there are set rules is wrong. But learn them before you break them!

PART 4

EDITORS

CHAPTER 9

GETTING AN EDITOR

At some point you will need to acquire feedback.

This could be from a paid editor, or it could be from another creative writing specialist, or even a friend – so long as they will be unbiased, brutal, and know what they are talking about.

A developmental editor is often the best way to get good advice. If you are traditionally published, this will often be sorted out for you. If you are independently publishing, this will be something you need to fund yourself.

Even if you are looking to get traditionally published, however, I would still get some feedback before you send your manuscript out.

A professional, experienced person will show you many problems you haven't picked up on. Even after publishing thirty novels, there are still problems introduced to me in the editing process that I would not have thought of, though most appear obvious once pointed out to me.

Remember, once you charge people money for your book, it is no longer a hobby – it is a business. Your book is no longer your piece of passion and art, it is a product. It is important you produce the best product possible.

Kellogg's would never release a pack of inadequate Frosties and say, "Well, it's fine it's not perfect, as it's art."

So, with this in mind, let's just run through what the different editors do.

Developmental Editors

A developmental editor looks at your story, considering the structure, plot, pace, characters and overall writing.

They then provide a report, usually 5-10 pages of A4. It is your job to selectively use their feedback to improve your work.

This will generally cost £500–1000 if you source it yourself, dependent upon length. I offer this service at www.bloodsplatterpress.com for horror or thriller writers. Alternatively, I have use a website called Writer's Workshop, where they will assign their own editor best suited to your genre, or Reedsy where you can put an advert out yourself.

Copy Editor

Your copy editor does not give you feedback on your characterisation or story. They give feedback on your grammar, spelling, sentence structure and word use.

A good copy editor will also notice things that aren't consistent throughout.

Copy editors are experts in syntax and word use – without one, you can expect to get bad reviews.

For example, I've done my best to eradicate typos from this book (although I am sure you may spot one – please email me if you do, I am always happy to know so I can get rid of it!) but if this book was ridden with typo after typo after typo, then it would lower the integrity of what I'm saying, wouldn't it?

I use a website called FirstEditing, or place an advert on Reedsy. Again, you can expect to spend £400-1000, dependent upon length.

Proof-reader

This is a person who does the final check for spelling, grammar and typos before publishing. They are like copy editors, except less detailed, and sometimes less qualified.

They look for obvious errors.

I offer this service at www.bloodsplatterpress.com, or you could acquire one on Reedsy, and they can cost £200-500. Sometimes, however, I pay an English student around £100 instead!

Advance Reader Team

This is something you may want to set up once you've published a book or two and are a little more established.

This is a team of fans who read my book a few weeks before publication. They let me know of any typos they spot and any glaring errors. They also help to fill the product page for my books with customer reviews before they launch.

This is free! Normally fans love to receive a free book before it's released, and it costs nothing to send it to their Kindle directly.

What's next?

Once you are ready for feedback, have a look at some of the websites I have given you. Research the cost of the editor, and what the editor offers.

Is there an editor you feel you could work with?

If so, get in touch, ask them any questions you have. Chances are, if they want your business, they will be happy to help.

CHAPTER 10

RESPONDING TO A DEVELOPMENTAL EDITOR'S FEEDBACK

So, you've given your book to a developmental editor, and they've sent you a document outlining their feedback.

Now what?

You now have a lot of information to go through and pick out.

Here are a few screenshots from some reports from one of my earlier books to give you some idea what they may say:

something that will genuinely thrill and unnerve your readers.

I hope that this report helps in that regard, and wish you the best moving forward (and very nice to see the first instalment has had a decent response in Amazon reviews).

COMMERCIAL POTENTIAL

Genre

As we discussed, the horror genre is one that is ripe for the picking. My only concern with this series and with this entry is that you occasionally call back to tropes without adding anything absolutely unique that we haven't seen before. I think you can do it; you just need to let go a little and think about doing things with the exorcisms scenes no one has done before, taking it from solid to memorable.

Local Flavour

Again, I think a bit more Brit grit flavour is needed. Horror thrives on taking the everday and making it unusual, so some more specific local details and flavour (names of pubs, streets, halls of Residence etc) could help. The BBC references were the only real clue to me that this was a British novel.

STRUCTURE AND PLOT

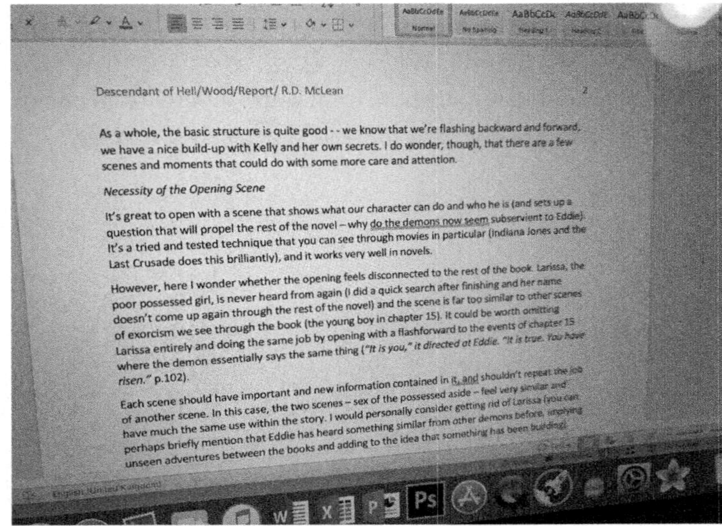

Descendant of Hell/Wood/Report/ R.D. McLean 2

As a whole, the basic structure is quite good - - we know that we're flashing backward and forward, we have a nice build-up with Kelly and her own secrets. I do wonder, though, that there are a few scenes and moments that could do with some more care and attention.

Necessity of the Opening Scene

It's great to open with a scene that shows what our character can do and who he is (and sets up a question that will propel the rest of the novel – why do the demons now seem subservient to Eddie). It's a tried and tested technique that you can see through movies in particular (Indiana Jones and the Last Crusade does this brilliantly), and it works very well in novels.

However, here I wonder whether the opening feels disconnected to the rest of the book. Larissa, the poor possessed girl, is never heard from again (I did a quick search after finishing and her name doesn't come up again through the rest of the novel) and the scene is far too similar to other scenes of exorcism we see through the book (the young boy in chapter 15). It could be worth omitting Larissa entirely and doing the same job by opening with a flashforward to the events of chapter 15 where the demon essentially says the same thing (*"It is you," it directed at Eddie. "It is true. You have risen."* p.102).

Each scene should have important and new information contained in it, and shouldn't repeat the job of another scene. In this case, the two scenes – sex of the possessed aside – feel very similar and have much the same use within the story. I would personally consider getting rid of Larissa (you can perhaps briefly mention that Eddie has heard something similar from other demons before, implying unseen adventures between the books and adding to the idea that something has been building)

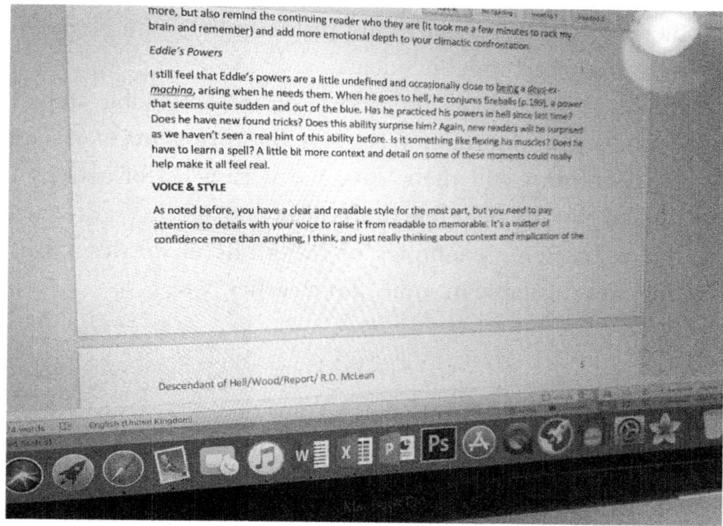

more, but also remind the continuing reader who they are (it took me a few minutes to rack my brain and remember) and add more emotional depth to your climactic confrontation.

Eddie's Powers

I still feel that Eddie's powers are a little undefined and occasionally close to being a *deus-ex machina*, arising when he needs them. When he goes to hell, he conjures fireballs (p.199), a power that seems quite sudden and out of the blue. Has he practiced his powers in hell since last time? Does he have new found tricks? Does this ability surprise him? Again, new readers will be surprised as we haven't seen a real hint of this ability before. Is it something like flexing his muscles? Does he have to learn a spell? A little bit more context and detail on some of these moments could really help make it all feel real.

VOICE & STYLE

As noted before, you have a clear and readable style for the most part, but you need to pay attention to details with your voice to raise it from readable to memorable. It's a matter of confidence more than anything, I think, and just really thinking about context and implication of the

Descendant of Hell/Wood/Report/ R.D. McLean

This tells me what isn't working, but I have not yet had any way to figure out what to do about it. It's just a lot of analysis being thrown at me.

The best way, I find, is to organise my thoughts with a table.

I will make three columns with the following headings:

- Area of Improvement.
- Ideas.
- Specific Improvements to Make.

First, I will fill my *Area of Improvement* column by going through my report and picking out all the things that I need to take action on. I will sum them up and note them down here.

Following this, I will come up with *Ideas* how to solve this problem. This is my opportunity just to bullet point all possibilities, and not to omit any ideas.

I look at these ideas and decide on the actionable steps I need to take and put them in *Specific Improvements to Make.*

This column will then leave me with a list of actions I need to take in the next few drafts of my novel.

Here are some examples of the kinds of entries I was making into this table in some of my earlier books:

Area of Improvement

- Change exorcism scenes to make different to existing exorcism scenes. Add originality. Particularly in opening and chapter 15.
- Nature of possession is cyclical and predictable. When Eddie encounters demons this often, I need to create new and unpredictable opponents.

Ideas

- Make first one be up the tree
- The next one in a different location. Garden? Cramped attic? Garden shed? Graveyard? Airplane? Helicopter as they try to take them to somewhere, has to do the exorcism straight away? (Could make for a very tense scene.)
- What would be a weird place to have an exorcism?
- (Bring Jenny and Lacy along to see?)
- They both have similar fits; change this.

- Laughter repeats; change this. Could one demon be in awe rather than smug? Beg for him to lead him? (Would make his roots even more blatant?)
- Highlight difference in demons: bargaining? Subservient? Tricksters?
- Add some new aspects that the reader doesn't expect. (See editor reference to Hellblazer.) Take a unique spin on exorcisms that's not been so far.
- Focus on specific sensory impressions to create difference: smells of the room, different kinds of cold.
- Eddie could try different ways of getting rid of the demons: various religious artefacts? Particular spells to use against certain demons? (Could have a specific one in opening scene – show difference in Eddie's approach, research he has had to do – could then show this research to prepare for his later exorcism?)

Specific Improvements to Make

- Change opening exorcism so they see the girl run out of the house and go to the garden shed, and they have to perform the exorcism there.
- Find an organic reason to them having to escort chapter 15 exorcism to another location; he is in another home, and they need to perform the exorcism in his own home so they can access the child with a place that is familiar. They get a helicopter over there and the demon reveals itself, breaking out of the restrains. Eddie says "we can't

wait any longer. We have to perform the exorcism now." He does it on the helicopter.

- Need to add reference to Derek's friend with a chopper earlier on
- Stop chapter 15 from having an exorcism and take away laughter. Make him more humble in sight of Eddie, begging for him to lead him. As Eddie refuses, he then turns psychotic.
- Show earlier scene where he tries out a new technique where he repels a demon out through channeling his gift through the possessed's chest, instead of using religious talk. (suddenly realises what he was doing wrong the other time)
- He finds religious talk doesn't work and is forced to use something stronger, as they don't have the familiar surroundings needed to help the trapped fight; so he puts his new gift into action. He doubts his ability as he has only tried it to get secrets out of people who aren't possessed; but Derek's encouragement gives him the push he needs to succeed.
- Add more references to the senses, what is around, in the exorcism scenes. Add some originality to the sights and smells Eddie experiences.

And, another:

Area of Improvement

- Connection to Jenny and Lacy isn't there when they are threatened, we need to see more of them early on.

Ideas

- Add scenes earlier on of them together, showing connection.
- How could I do this and ensure it isn't a scene for the sake of it? Make it drive the story along?
- (Could they attend the exorcism?)

Specific Improvements to Make

- Have him practising his gift with Jenny and Lacy, of withdrawing hidden secrets from them with channelling his powers into the chest; which he will do to succeed later on in chapter 15 exorcism. He fails first few times, then gets something final. Highlights to them afterwards when they are impressed that it's a very small scale, and it will take more practice for him to do it in an exorcism.
- He enlists Jenny's help in helping him conjure fireballs (and other things) using a spell book for the gifted following the success of chapter 15. He fails, though.
- He tries again, Jenny rereading the spell and

looking at something they didn't do. He chants the incantation and tries again. Fails.

- Jenny looks at Eddie and thinks about whether she has seen these powers in him at all before; show an earlier scene when they were kids, emphasising the strong friendship, when he somehow helps her from a bully without even realising.

What's next?

Once you have your feedback ready, read through it, getting a sense of what your editor has said. Remember to take all their suggestions in the constructive way they meant it.

(The first editor report I ever had said, "Well done for writing a book." When that's the praise your editor gives you, you know you have a lot of work ahead!)

Now use this table to organise your thoughts and reactions. Create some actionable steps you can use to take your book to the finishing stage.

PART 5

WHAT TO DO AFTER YOU'VE FINISHED

CHAPTER 11

TRADITIONAL VS INDEPENDENT PUBLISHING

Congratulations, you have finished your book!

Or, if you are reading this before you've finished... congratulations, you will at some point finish your book!

The next step is to decide what to do with it.

The two routes are traditional or independent publishing. Let's have a look at the definition of what they mean:

Traditional Publishing: This is when you send your book out to agents. Eventually, an agent signs you, and they attempt to sell your book to a publisher who then works on your book and distributes it. This is the way it has been done for a long, long time.

Independent Publishing: This is when you publish your book yourself through Amazon and, should you choose, various other platforms such as Kobo, Barnes and Noble and Apple Books. This is a more recent way of publishing and has divided writers and publishers in their opinions.

Of course, I will approach this with a certain bias. I have independently published and have made a great career for myself through doing so, and I know of a lot of other independent authors who are making huge amounts of money. Yes, I have had to learn how to market my books – but at least I am in control of my book's success.

Honestly, there is no chance I would have had the success I've had if I went down the traditional route. Chances are, I would still be seeking an agent. Even if I'd acquired one, I may have released one, maybe two books, which would have likely been published to obscurity. Unfortunately, most traditionally published books are not *Harry Potter*. Most don't do that well.

That being said, you can't just independently publish a book and expect it to do well. You have to learn about marketing.

I dreaded learning about marketing as I considered myself to have no business sense. Now, I enjoy the marketing just as much as I enjoy the writing.

I will, however, try to remove any bias, and look analytically at both sides of the argument. Here are the pros and cons of each:

The Advantages of Traditional Publishing

This side of publishing holds more integrity. People in the industry, whether rightly or wrongly, often see it as the place that 'real' writers go.

There is less financial investment for you. Covers, editing and marketing is taken care of by someone else.

There is more potential to achieve a literary award. It is rare to see an independently published book win one of the major literary awards.

. . .

The Disadvantages of Traditional Publishing

Even though the marketing is taken care of by the publisher, you are still, realistically, going to have to do a substantial amount of publicity yourself, such as social media or running a mailing list.

It is far tougher to make a living; you have less control, and smaller royalty rates on your book.

There is also a timescale. As an indie author, I can release a book whenever I want. A traditional author will be limited to one or two a year.

The major drawback of this route is the 'gatekeepers.' You have to go through a lot of hurdles to get traditionally published. The quality of your book is second to its marketability, and publishers are not likely to take a risk.

The Advantages of Independently Publishing

There is more potential to make a living, because you are in control and have far higher royalty rates.

The amount of success you have is not down to the department of a publishing house where your book is one of many. The success is all down to you.

The Disadvantages of Independently Publishing

There is a significant amount of financial investment and risk, especially if you want to see a good amount of people read your book.

There is also a steep learning curve, and it takes time and money to learn how to market.

The biggest drawback is the stigma attached. Many still believe this to be second choice, for those who cannot achieve a publishing deal. Even indie authors earning six or seven figures a year admit to having a slight inferiority complex. I believe this is because a lot of independently published authors release their books without professional editing. This results in a judgement on all independently published books, and those of us who do ensure we do publish a professional product have to deal with that.

What next?

There is no right or wrong route, only what is best for you.

Consider the advantages and disadvantages laid out for you in this chapter. Decide what your idea of success is. Do you want to make a living? Or do you just want to finish a book and have a few people read it?

Ultimately, you must decide which route is best for you.

CHAPTER 12

INDEPENDENTLY PUBLISHING

I WILL NOT GO INTO DETAIL ABOUT HOW TO MAKE A living as an indie author. It is far beyond the scope of this book, and there are many books and courses out there ready to help. I would suggest looking up the courses by Mark Dawson, or the books by Joanna Penn, should you wish to learn how to market.

I will, however, just touch on where and how I advertise to make my money.

Mailing List

The most important part of any author's marketing. The first thing you see after reading any of my books is a link to my mailing list, along with the promise of a free book should you join. The book is usually a novella within the genre, or to do with the series they have just read.

I engage my mailing list with weekly emails, though you don't have to email that often. Personally, I like to engage my readers with interesting content so when I send them an email saying my book is out; they are more likely to open it.

I would suggest reading *Newsletter Ninja* by Tammi L. Labrecque to learn how to successfully engage your mailing list.

Amazon Marketing Services

Amazon have their own platform for marketing.

When looking for a book on Amazon, you may type the title or genre of the book you are looking for into the search. I bid against other authors for my book to appear once you have searched for certain keywords.

For example, I bid on the keyword search 'paranormal horror book' with *The Sensitives*.

You can also advertise your books on the product pages of books similar to yours.

Facebook Advertising

Some indie authors swear by this, some don't.

Personally, I have found it ineffective for my horror books, but very effective for my thriller books.

You can create adverts that target people with various interests, as well as targeting specific people. For example, when I have a new book out, I load the email addresses of my mailing list into Facebook Advertising, who then finds the accounts attached to those email addresses, and I target adverts for my new book at them.

You can also advertise for people to join your mailing list.

BookBub Advertising

BookBub are a company that send daily emails of book offers to a responsive audience. There are many companies that do this, such as Bargain Booksy or Fussy Librarian. BookBub is the most effective.

You can apply to pay for your book to feature in their email. These are called Featured Deals and are difficult to get. Alternatively, you can bid for your advert to appear at the bottom of their email.

What next?

If you are considering independent publishing, do some research into the various platforms you can publish on, ways of publishing, and the key figures in indie publishing that you can follow.

There are many YouTube videos, books and courses out there. Just start searching!

CHAPTER 13

TRADITIONAL PUBLISHING

So you've decided to try to get traditionally published.

Publishers are unlikely to accept submissions if they are not from an agent. So, the first thing you need to do is acquire an agent.

Research agents who manage authors in your genre. Use Google. Use *The Writers and Artists Handbook* – a book that is released every year with lists of agents in. Use word of mouth if you can.

Once you've found an appropriate agent, send them a query letter and your manuscript. Before you do this, make sure you look at what that agent specifically asks for in a submission. Some want a ten-page sample. Some want a treatment. If you do not send them what they have requested, chances are your submission will go straight in the bin.

They may also ask for specific detail in your query letter. If this is not the case, however, this is the information a query letter will normally include:

- Format as you would a normal letter

- Introduce yourself with a short biography. Is there anything interesting or enticing you can say about yourself? I emphasise that this should be short. You don't need to tell them every detail of your mother's introduction to parenthood, your subsequent birth and every year that followed. Do consider your genre though. If you have written a comedy, then make it fun. If you have written a horror, add a little mysteriousness.
- A brief overview of your story. This is basically your character, the situation and the problem.
- Tell the agent why you are interested in signing with them. For example, *I've noticed that you are <author>'s agent, and I see my books as having a similar market.*
- Finish with a final selling paragraph.

Again, different agents will say what they want to see in terms of your manuscript. If they do not, this is the standard:

- A synopsis.
- A sample of the manuscript (if they want to read more, they will ask for it.)

Do remember that an agent works for you, not the other way around. Don't go for the wrong agent out of desperation. I've known authors be elated to get signed, who then spent the next twenty years only having published the one book that has disappeared into obscurity.

Expect to get rejected. In fact, expect it a lot. It's about persistence. And, in the unlikely event that the agent gives you feedback, use it. Tweak your manuscript every time.

Here are some common reasons an agent may reject you:

- You have not followed their submission instructions.
- They do not see your book or genre as marketable.
- You have not shown evidence of researching the agent.
- Your formatting is not correct.

With formatting your manuscript, the agent may specify what they are after. If they don't, the standard is twelve-point Times New Roman, double spaced with numbered pages.

Send out your work, but don't hold your breath.

Keep learning and keep trying.

If it takes eighty times, it takes eighty.

If it takes thousands, it takes thousands.

Save your rejection letters. Use them as motivation.

Someday you may be able to show your fans how many times your book was rejected.

And good luck!

What's next?

Research agents in your genre. Research the agents of authors similar to you. Research, research, research.

Then draft a letter. Look over it. Look over it again. Get feedback on it and redraft it just as you would a book.

Finally, and most importantly, grow a thick skin. The thickest. Be impenetrable to rejection, but open to advice.

As I have said already, the fear of mistakes is the enemy of creativity.

AFTERWORD

There you go. A concise book of all that I have learned in the four years since I published my first book.

Although, it's not just been four years and thirty odd books, has it?

When I was a child, I would spend my summer afternoons on my dad's Windows 95 computer, bashing away at the word processer.

When I was sixteen, I bought my own computer. I attended an evening course on scriptwriting. I spent my nights, when other teenagers were out partying as I probably should have been doing, bashing away at my latest story.

They were all awful.

I wrote my first story at seven.

I published my first at twenty-eight.

If you take twenty-one years, then you took the same time as I did.

Of course, there's also a degree in Scriptwriting in there. A master's in Creative Writing. A PhD in Literary and Critical Studies that, at the time of publishing this book, I have just begun.

Not that you require such qualifications to write. Most who do don't. It simply demonstrates that my thirst for knowledge never ended. Even after five bestsellers, being able to give up my day job, and thirty-odd novels, I am still seeking ways to learn.

Every book I write ends up being better than the last. That is the result. And that is what you should aim for.

In fact, if I am honest with you, when I read my first book series back, *The Edward King Series,* I cringe. Compared to what I write now, it is awful. Abysmal.

That series grew me a fanbase, yes, but honestly, I have since let that series disappear into obscurity. I have let the lesser versions of my writing fade away with lack of marketing and advertising, hoping that new fans will stick to my newer, better work.

In three years from now, however, I am sure I will look back at the books I have just written and feel the same way.

So never rue a mistake. Never cease gaining new skills and new knowledge. Do not see yourself as failing, but progressing.

You need to remove the fear of failure and of writing something awful. Pretty much everyone who's tried writing a book and not finished has cited despair at what they've written as an excuse.

Write, then rewrite, then learn new skills and write again.

Mine is not the only book out there.

My opinion is not the only opinion.

So seek more. Tell me I'm right, tell me I'm wrong, whatever – just be able to back it up.

Whatever you say, though, never claim you are awful.

A defeatist attitude is the enemy of all aspiring writers. Those who achieve what I have are simply the ones who conquer doubt.

And, with that final dose of learning, I will depart.
After all, why are you still reading this, anyway?
The book is done.
It's time for you to get writing.

NEED HELP WITH YOUR BOOK?

We offer many services to horror and thriller authors to help you publish your book, including:

- Developmental Editing
- Proofreading
- Cover Design
- Advertising Graphics

For more information, please visit www.bloodsplatterpress.com

ALSO BY RICK WOOD

The Sensitives:

Book One – The Sensitives

Book Two – My Exorcism Killed Me

Book Three – Close to Death

Book Four – Demon's Daughter

Book Five – Questions for the Devil

Book Six - Repent

Book Seven - The Resurgence

Book Eight - Until the End

Shutter House

Shutter House

Prequel Book One - This Book is Full of Bodies

Cia Rose:

Book One – After the Devil Has Won

Book Two – After the End Has Begun

Book Three - After the Living Have Lost

Chronicles of the Infected

Book One – Zombie Attack

Book Two – Zombie Defence

Book Three – Zombie World

Standalones:

When Liberty Dies

I Do Not Belong

Death of the Honeymoon

Sean Mallon:

Book One – The Art of Murder

Book Two – Redemption of the Hopeless

The Edward King Series:

Book One – I Have the Sight

Book Two – Descendant of Hell

Book Three – An Exorcist Possessed

Book Four – Blood of Hope

Book Five – The World Ends Tonight

Non-Fiction

How to Write an Awesome Novel

Thrillers published as Ed Grace:

The Jay Sullivan Thriller Series

Assassin Down

Kill Them Quickly

Printed in Great Britain
by Amazon

41716474R00078